CUBA

We would particularly like to thank Françoise Dubois Sigmund of AOM,
Una Liutkus of Havanatour and especially Rosa Adela Mesias from the Cuban Tourist Office in Paris
for their amiable welcome and valuable help.

EVERGREEN is an imprint of Benedikt Taschen Verlag GmbH

© for this edition: 1999 Benedikt Taschen Verlag GmbH
Hohenzollernring 53, D–50672 Köln
© 1998 Editions du Chêne – Hachette Livre – Cuba
Under the direction of Michel Buntz – Hoa Qui Photographic Agency
Text: Franc Nichele
Photographs: Michel Renaudeau/Hoa Qui
(except: page 107 Olivier Beytout; page 73 top P. de Wilde; pages 13 and 72 top V. Durruty;
pages 51 top, 72 bottom, 73 bottom and 90 top P. Guedj; page 47 Franc Nichele; pages 102 left and 138 A. Perigot;
pages 24, 58, 59 top, 112 and 151 B. Pérousse; pages 14, 22 top, 46 top, 68 left, 137 bottom and 142 Julien Quideau;
pages 145, 146, 147, 148, 149 and 150 Guido Alberto Rossi;
pages 67, 114 and 115 Philippe Roy; page 106 Christophe Valentin.
Photographs supplied by the Hoa Qui Photographic Agency.)
Layout: Roger Donadini
Map and illustrations: Jean-Michel Kirsch
Editor: Corinne Fossey
Cover design: Angelika Taschen, Cologne
Translated by Ian West
In association with First Edition Translations Ltd, Cambridge
Realisation of the English edition by First Edition Translations Ltd, Cambridge

Printed in Italy
ISBN 3-8228-7064-1

CUBA

Text FRANC NICHELE
Photographs MICHEL RENAUDEAU

EVERGREEN

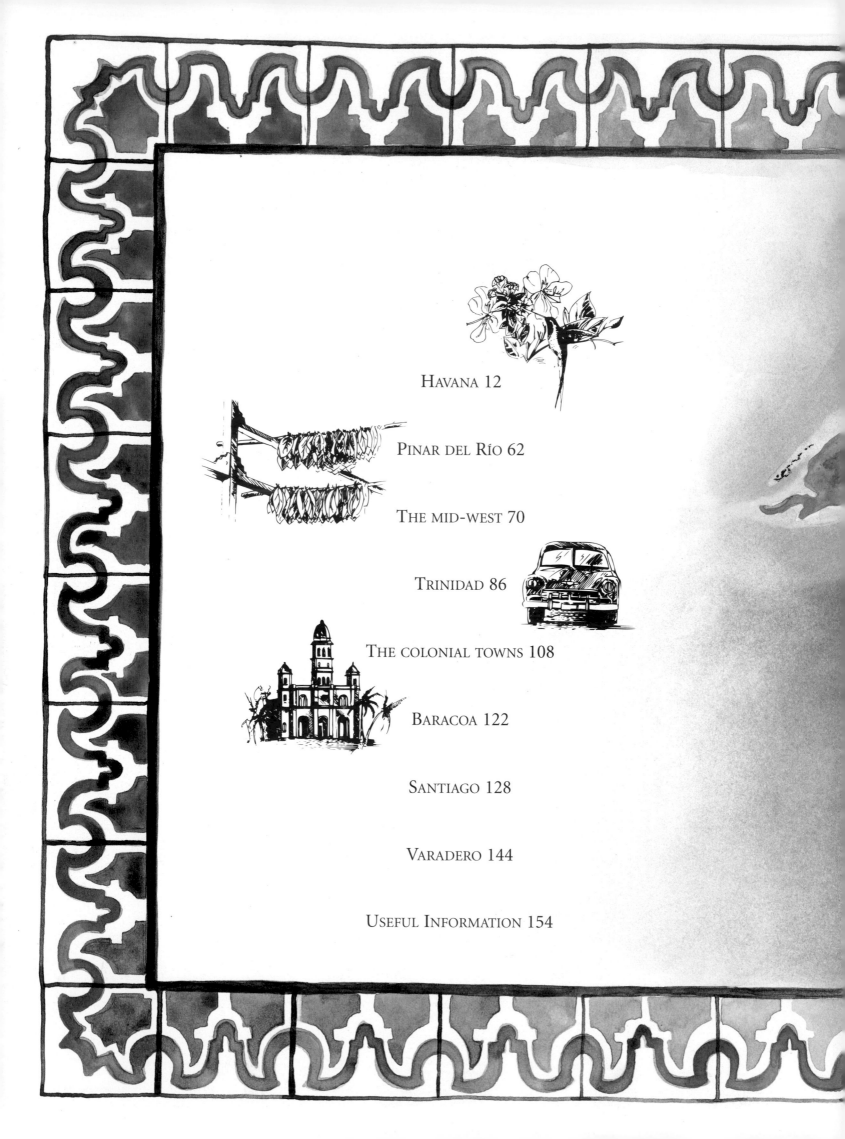

THE TWO FACES OF PARADISE

Cuba is a land where grandeur rubs shoulders with decline. The paradise is real enough, but sometimes it leaves a bitter taste. A country cannot escape unscathed from thirty-five years of communism: hence the paradox. But paradise there is. To prove the point, just make a short trip from Florida, in the direction of Yucatán. To the Tropic of Cancer, at the entrance to the Gulf of Mexico, to be precise, where you will find yourself on an island four times as big as Sicily. The textbooks tell us that Cuba has a total area – including offshore islands – of nearly 111,111 km² (42,900 sq miles), that it is shaped like a crocodile, and that the beast measures 1,250 kilometres (781 miles) from head to tail. At its widest, it is less than 200 kilometres (125 miles) across. So much for mere dimensions. From the glamour angle, Cuba can boast 2,600 kilometres (1,625 miles) of beaches, 4,200 coral reefs, and 425 kilometres (266 miles) of mountains. At the start of the nineteenth century, tropical forest covered ninety per cent of the territory. Today, the total is only a fraction of this, but Cuba remains the island of palm trees – particularly the royal palm, which is one of the country's emblems. Sugar cane grows everywhere, alongside tobacco, coffee, rice, and citrus fruits. There are deposits of nickel, copper, and iron – also some oil. Today, tourism is the leading industry in Cuba, with a million visitors a year and three million expected in the year 2000.

Side by side with Haiti, Cuba has one of the richest and most dramatic histories of all the Caribbean islands. In 1511 or 1512 the conquistador Diego Velázquez de Cuéllar, on the orders of the Spanish crown, landed on the island, then known as Juana in honour of Prince Juan of Spain. By 1514, the conquest was complete – Velázquez had founded seven towns and massacred ninety per cent of the native

Indian population. The trade in Negro slaves began in 1524. The slave-trade, sugar cane and coffee plantations, and the constant traffic of galleons in and out of the port of Havana, turned Cuba into the wealthiest and most developed island of the Antilles.

Such was the state of affairs till the end of the eighteenth century, when Creoles and slaves alike began to dream of some sort of independence. A man rose to the occasion – Carlos Manuel de Céspedes – a rebel planter, who organized the First War of Independence (1868), later known as the Ten Years War. He died in battle, and his banner passed to his comrade-in-arms, Antonio Maceo. These were two of the earliest legendary figures in Cuba's history. A few years later, José Martí was to appear on the scene as the hero of the Second War of Independence, which led to 55,000 Spanish deaths and, in 1898, to the intervention of the United States. The Platt Amendment proved to be nothing other than an American annexation of Cuba. The American occupation was to last three years, at the end of which the first Cuban president was nominated: Tomás Estrada Palma. From then on, one president after another – some corrupt, some mere puppets, some both – followed in a rapid succession of coups, counter-coups, and dictatorships. In 1909 Miguel Gómez took office; his nickname was Pépé the Shark. In 1913 it was the turn of General García Menocal, who tumbled at the same time as the price of sugar. In 1925 General Gerardo Machado installed a venal, brutal, and authoritarian regime. There was a short-lived attempt at democracy in 1933 under the leadership of the progressive Rámon Grau San Martín. Another coup followed. In 1940, an obscure colonel by the name of Fulgencio Batista contrived to win the elections. Four years later, he had to make way for the return of Grau San Martín, who, after one mandate, was ousted by Carlos Prío Socarrás. Then in 1952,

*O*verleaf:
These karstic formations – limestone monoliths known as 'mogotes' – are only to be found in Cuba and China. The landscapes round Viñales, west of Havana and close to Pinar del Río (Pine Forest by the River), are amongst the most impressive in the Antilles.

Batista returned to power via a military revolt, and remained for six years till the Revolution.

The rest of the story belongs to more recent times, from the abortive Bay of Pigs invasion by exiled Cubans, through the 1962 missile crisis – when the world trembled on the brink of nuclear war – up to the disintegration of the Soviet Union and the cessation of economic and financial aid from Big Brother to its turbulent Caribbean ally. But contrary to all expectations, and despite a senseless American embargo serving only to reduce the people to starvation without persuading them to rebel, the country's economy has gradually rallied since 1995, and there is even talk of new growth. This is essentially due to tourism and its related industries. Now European countries invest in Cuba, despite American threats and the Helms-Burton legislation penalizing all trade between Cuba and the West. So, in 1990, Cuba opened her doors to the world, somewhat grudgingly and reluctantly, after thirty years of seclusion and ideological isolation. As for the Cubans, they are not complaining – especially the young, hungry to know for the first time what is actually happening on the rest of the planet. Tourists give them a somewhat false impression. They see a holiday-maker with pocketfuls of dollars, without considering that even millionaires have their limits. Of course, for a Cuban sick of queueing outside shops with his or her libreta (ration book), anything which is bought for dollars is relatively expensive. Especially if you consider that a doctor's salary is at most $30 a month, paid in pesos. On the other hand, a porter in a big hotel is entitled to a dollar or so each time he carries the suitcases up to a bedroom! This wage gap is an increasing source of unrest amongst key workers outside the tourist sector.

The 'santera', always dressed in white, symbolizing purity, is both a priestess of the santería cult and a healer of all ills – including bad luck. People consult her to win the favour of the 'saints'.

Havana is one of

the two or three cities

in the world whose reality

surpasses its reputation.

Magnificent
HAVANA

Any foregone conclusions about Havana are bound to turn out to be wrong. Everything you have read or been told, all the pictures you have seen, you need to multiply five, ten times over to get somewhere near the truth. And that is only a start! Havana is one of the two or three cities in the world whose reality surpasses its reputation.

On a humid tropical day, you arrive at the airport and start out on the long, tedious road leading to the the capital. At once, you get an instinctive feeling you are about to make the acquaintance of an exceptional, astonishing, breathtaking city – but also one hell-bent on self-destruction. You will be dazzled, beguiled, and infuriated, all at the same time. You can expect adventures in the true sense of the word, with strange, exciting things just waiting to happen.

Havana gives off an aura of power and vibrancy rather than sheer beauty: that is what makes it special. One instance of its power is the weather – sometimes mild and breezy, sometimes violently oppressive in the 35°C (95°F) heat of July and August. Storms about to break over the city give the impression of an approaching cataclysm. Everything turns dark. The thunder cracks like a whiplash overhead, and lightning often strikes the roofs. When the sea is roused, waves

Balconies and terraces are an integral part of Cubans' social life. They use them to enjoy the fresh air, dry their washing, watch television, or play music.

burst 3 metres (9–10 ft) over the wall of the Malecón – the seafront highway – and swipe passing cars. On windy days, windows shatter and draughts become hurricanes. Rain here comes Hollywood-style: pedestrians are drenched to the skin immediately. But when the weather is calm, the wind off the sea is like a breath or a caress.

A kind of Caribbean Babylon, Havana long ago made her pact with all the gods and devils of creation. Havana the corrupt, Havana the scarlet woman, battered and bruised by fate, submissive, loving, she nevertheless always rises from her ruins. She is the femme fatale, once beautiful to excess, but still with fantastic class, despite all her troubles. Sensual, tropical, decadent, the half-caste offspring of Florida and Spanish America, Havana goes on for ever.

ON THE 'PROM', HAVANA-STYLE

There is only one way to start your visit to Havana. First climb into one of the open-top taxis at the beginning of the Malecón, then get

the driver to cruise slowly along its 5-kilometre (3-mile) length just when the sun is going down over the sea, opposite the city. The evening is steeped in radiance. Twilight on the seafront here has the feel of an American night, when the washed-out colours of the colonnaded houses merge with the pastel dresses of passing girls. The Malecón serves as an immense terrace overlooking the Straits of Florida. As the light fades, the promenade wall becomes the gathering-place for all Havana. Habaneros bring along music – guitars perhaps – and definitely bottles of rum. Rum to brighten up the night, even if it is the bad stuff locals call *chispa de tren* – train sparks! On public holidays, when the Malecón is closed to traffic, the sea wall quite literally turns into a series of auditoriums, and groups form at certain strategic places – La Piragua, for instance, in front of the Hotel Nacional de Cuba, or La Fuente outside the Riviera. The Riviera is a luxury hotel built forty-odd years ago by the American Mafia boss Meyer-Lanski, and now a faded monument to the glory of

Life is lived on the street. In Habana Vieja, domino players sit at outdoor tables. The pinkish walls are those of the Ambos Mundos Hotel, recently renovated.
Overleaf:
Young girls dressed for carnival in Havana (July).

the 1950s. It looks for all the world like the set for a spy film. The Malecón finally disappears under the Miramar tunnel – not without a certain flourish, since the sea wall stops at Restaurante 1830, a magnificent mansion where you can eat and dance in a curious, Japanese-style garden. Quite indifferent to all this, amateur fishermen sit in the water in huge inflated inner-tubes, dozing rather than fishing.

UP-MARKET HAVANA

On the other side of the tunnel begins Fifth Avenue (Avenida 5) and the district of Miramar, the ultra-chic quarter of the Batista days and still a residential area. The candy-pink villas and the little tropical-deco mansions rub shoulders with all the embassies and numerous state-controlled businesses. A large and magnificent white building,

familiarly known as The House, lurks amongst the trees. If luxury and beauty are bourgeois conceptions, this place cocks an enormous snook at Latin-American socialism. The former aristocratic residence conceals fashionable shops, an open-air bar and restaurant, and a swimming pool. Every night at half past ten, in what is the Mecca of Cuban high society, you can witness a parade of fifteen or so of what must be the most gorgeous showgirls in the entire capital. Once, all the villas in the Miramar district had pools, since the beaches consisted of nothing but sheer, black rocks. Now, the pools are empty and the beach is the same. Moving a bit further on, you come to Siboney, which is more modern than Miramar. Fine, big mansions are secreted within leafy parks. It is here, amongst other places, that Fidel Castro lives – actually, he is said to own half a dozen homes in Havana, and no one is ever exactly sure where he is.

If you really want swimming and sunbathing, the best place is 20 kilometres (12½ miles) from Havana, on the string of beaches known

The Parque Central is one of Havana's most popular spots. The 'classical' architecture may be revival – big nineteenth-century hotels reminiscent of the Italian Riviera – but it is unmistakeably Old Havana.

*T*he restoration of Havana's
buildings has been going strong
for several years – a colossal task,
led by teams of architects and
students, with work now in
progress on over sixty buildings.

*E*ye-catching American cars dating from the 1950s are used as taxis.
Tourists prefer them to Soviet-built Ladas.
Opposite: The Capitol, similar to that in Washington, inaugurated in 1929.
Before the Revolution, it housed the Chamber of Deputies and the Senate.

• Those American beauties •

Needless to say, as soon as tourists set eyes on these chrome-laden treasures of the 1950s cruising Havana's streets, they wanted to buy them up and take them home. No way! was Fidel's reply. They were, he said, part of the national heritage. They can only be bought if they stay in the country. A 1959 Chevrolet Bel Air fetches between £1,000 and £1,500. Probably there are more cars from that era in Cuba than in the States. Anyone lucky enough to have patched one up and kept it going for the last thirty years is sitting on a goldmine – Cubans use them as taxis, and the tourists love them. Quite recently, the government decided to create an organization for renovating these American beauties. Nowadays they are a real part of the Cuban scene: the place would not be the same without them. There are some 400,000 on the whole island – Chevrolet Bel Airs, Impalas, Oldsmobiles, Buicks, Chrysler Plymouths, Ford Victorias, and Thunderbirds ...

José Martí, father of the Revolution, is honoured in many public places in Havana and provincial towns. A visionary figure, he foresaw that after the Spanish colonization, the chief threat to his country would be America. He is Cuba's most respected historical figure.

as Las Playas del Este. However, if you want more peace and quiet, you can push on further to Guanabo beach, not far away. This is named after a coastal village where bungalows are rented on a daily basis. Everything here is geared to beach life, and it is a relaxing place after the clamminess of the capital.

VEDADO

Ernest Hemingway adored the turbulent Straits of Florida for their waters teeming with marlin. The sea can turn very violent overnight with the help of a small hurricane or two – it then boils over the

The Interior of Habana Vieja's cathedral, completed in 1787. The baroque façade of the former seminary of San Carlos and San Ambrosio.
Overleaf:
The cathedral of San Cristóbal de la Habana is open at specified times only, including the 10.30 mass on Sundays. The plaza is nowadays one of the most delightful places to sit and enjoy a relaxing evening drink.

parapet of the Malecón, flooding it and invading the nearest streets of Vedado. Vedado possesses tremendous charm: already a residential quarter in the thirties, it consists of a grid of long streets bordered by trees, villas, and small apartment blocks. But the whole area is gently crumbling away after thirty-five years of neglect. The boundaries of Vedado are two big parallel avenues leading right up to the Malecón: the Avenida de los Presidentes and the Paseo del Prado. The latter is particularly pleasant, with its central alleys shaded by fig trees, mango trees, and coral trees. The Paseo is intersected at right angles by the Rampa (officially part of Calle 23), one of Havana's largest boulevards, whose ambiance was once extremely *caliente* – raunchy – especially on the side where the big hotels were. In the early days of the Revolution, Fidel Castro occupied a whole floor of what was then the Hilton – this was the period when there was an attempt to poison him. The Rampa is both a commercial and a cultural artery, with cinemas, bookshops, and theatres. Towards its north-east end take the

SEMINARIO SAN CARLOS Y SAN AMBROSIO

• Hemingway's love affair with Cuba •

In 1939, Martha Gellhorn, Ernest Hemingway's third wife, discovered a hacienda (Finca Vigía) on the heights of San Francisco de Paula, some 15 kilometres (9 miles) from Havana, and with a spectacular view at night of the capital's lights. In 1940 Ernest bought it as a Christmas present for the two of them. The writer felt at home there, with his fifty or more cats, his den in a purpose-built tower, where he could write without being disturbed, his favourite armchair beside the drinks trolley, his hunting trophies, and his 9,000 books. He spent twenty years of his life there, till 1960, when he was already experimenting with a means to kill himself: he would place his hunting rifle in his mouth and pull the trigger with his toe. A year later, he did it for real, in Idaho.

Hemingway felt no urge to take sides either for or against the Revolution. He disliked Batista, but was unacquainted with Castro. For Hemingway, Cuba was truly a paradise island, where he loved to entertain his cronies, and where Ava Gardner swam naked in his pool. He was only a few miles away from his favourite bar-stool in the Floridita, where he read his newspaper while knocking back daiquiris, holding long discussions with the barmen, and occasionally punching an over-inquisitive journalist.

He first visited the Cuban coast to fish for marlin in the late 1920s when he was living at Key West. Then he began to go ashore more and more frequently, always staying at the Ambos Mundos Hotel and demanding the same top-floor room with its view over the port and Old Havana. It was there he wrote part of For Whom the Bell Tolls.

Hemingway had bought the Finca Vigía for just 12,500 dollars; Hollywood paid 125,000 for the rights to the short story The Snows of Kilimanjaro. There is still a tremendous presence in the house: it feels as if the great man must have just popped out. Visitors are not allowed inside; you have to look in through the windows. It was in Cuba that Hemingway learnt he had received the Nobel Prize for Literature, and his first interviews were given in this house. Asked why he loved Cuba so much, Hemingway's invariable reply was: 'It's just the way it is.'

*F*inca Vigía: 'Farm with a View' or 'Lookout Farm' – Hemingway's name for the hacienda on the hilltops of San Francisco de Paula, some 15 kilometres (9 miles) from Havana. In the drawing-room, notice the armchair on the left: Hemingway's habitual seat, within reach of the drinks.

Old mansions – particularly their courtyards – are frequently used as open-air restaurants, as at the former Palacio de los Marqueses de Aguas Claras, now El Patio, whose stained glass fanlights glow red and blue in the sunlight.
Preceding pages:
The Bodeguita del Medio, created by Ángel Martínez in 1942, became one of Havana's most fashionable bar-restaurants. Specialities are 'mojito' (a rum-based cocktail) and criollo cuisine.

southern branch of Avenue L. Where this swings east to become San Lázaro, you will see the massive stairway of the University of Havana. These steps were the scene of student demonstrations in the capital. Almost opposite, a monument has been erected in memory of the young communist assassinated in 1929, Julio Mella, founder of the Federation of Communist Students. The present university complex, built on a small hill, dates from the second quarter of this century. The quieter, more residential area of Vedado, with its chequerboard pattern of streets, begins lower down. Install yourself in one of the numerous guest-houses which have sprung up there over the last few years, and you will get a real taste of everyday life in Havana. The most striking feature of what is almost a piece of rural Cuba right in the heart of the city is the noise from the street. Noise, though, is not the right word: it is not what we hear in our great European cities. We should say *sounds*. The streets are full of sounds, but they are not noisy. Neighbours call out to each other. Instead of ringing the door-

bell, they shout the name of the person they have come to see. The last syllable of the name is drawn out, giving the effect of singing. Vendors, too, cry their wares in the streets, hawking all kinds of products – eggs, ham, fruit, vegetables – which they sell at the houses for *pesos Cubanos,* the national currency. Here, life is lived on the street. *Habaneros* also prefer to sit on the walls and balconies of their apartment blocks rather than inside, so they bring their rocking-chairs out of doors! Talking of rocking-chairs, the way people sprawl in them is typically Cuban: careless and sensuous. In Havana, music is also everywhere. Here you go to bed to music and wake up to music. If it is not your neighbours listening to it, there is always a band practising somewhere.

Upper-storey room and veranda: the Fototeca, where more than 25,000 archive photos of Cuba are stored.

We cannot leave Vedado without mentioning the Plaza de la Revolución. This could pass for a typically Stalinist symbol, yet it was originally constructed under Batista. Fidel Castro made a speech more than seven hours long here on 8 January 1959, after the victory of his *barbudos.* It was here too that the Pope celebrated Mass in 1998 before a crowd of 400,000. The sun always beats down mercilessly, and there are few strollers to be seen. Government buildings surround the Plaza on all sides, including those occupied by the Council of State and the Central Committee of the Cuban Communist Party. An immense portrait of Che has been affixed to the front of the Ministry of the Interior, complete with one of his most famous slogans: *Hasta la victoria siempre:* Ever Onwards to Victory.

A NOVEL WAY TO MOVE HOUSE

There is an avenue at right-angles to the first stage of the Malecón, unerringly straight, and shaded by umbrella trees and colonial-style houses. This is the *paseo* known as the Prado – walk along it and you

In the Palace of the Captains-General (Palacio de los Capitanes Generales) – now the Museo de la Ciudad – the celebrated snail-shaped bathtubs where Princess Eulalia of Bourbon bathed in 1893 can be seen.

The ceremonial rooms of this museum are often used as a backdrop for the 'coming-of-age' photo – an important occasion for teenage girls in Cuba, part of the rites of passage into adulthood.

A marble statue of Christopher Columbus adorns the museum courtyard.

will come to Habana Vieja, the historic quarter thronged with tourists. A carbon copy of the fine *paseos* in Andalusian or Catalonian towns, the Prado used to be the favourite promenading place for wealthy Cuban families. It has lost nothing of its charm, and its shady stone seats are always welcome after even a brief walk in the sun. Halfway along it rises the impressive mass of the Sevilla Hotel, built in 1880 in pure Andalusian style. Across the avenue the houses have a Moorish look; the architecture of some is completely oriental. In the mornings, the *paseo* serves as a playground for young schoolchildren in red uniforms and red scarves, romping under the watchful eye of short-skirted mistresses. In the afternoons, the alleys of the Prado become estate agencies. These are some of the most lively locations for the Cuban tradition of flat-trading. It is illegal to sell flats, and in any case most belong to the state; so *habaneros* swap them instead, and move house very cheaply. The process gives rise to interminable arguments, since rarely will two apartments be worth exactly the

• El Comandante Che Guevara •

It was on an evening in July 1955 that a certain Ernesto Guevara, an Argentinian Marxist revolutionary, met Fidel Castro in Mexico City. The latter was anxious to free his country from the tyrannical Batista, puppet of the North American Mafia. The two men talked all night; they made a pact to leave together on the same boat, conquer the island, and topple Cuba's mulatto dictator. Ernesto was 27, and had qualified as a doctor two years previously. Fidel Castro saw in him a very valuable ally, whilst Ernesto loved the idea of fighting against paid lackeys of the Yankees, whom he detested. The Granma expedition was a disaster, but the two men managed to escape to the foothills of the Sierra Maestra, where they were to set up a rudimentary form of communism. Ernesto, henceforth to be known as Che – from his typically Argentinian mannerism of littering his speech with the word che ('eh?' or 'hey!') – turned out to be a good doctor and a skilful teacher, setting up hospitals and schools. He was also unflappable in combat, a byword for heroism and courage. This he made plain during the attack on the armoured train at Santa Clara, a victory which sounded the death-knell for the loyalist forces. Che made a

triumphal entry into Havana in January 1959. The man was already a myth.

Fidel Castro found a use for him at the start of his period of leadership. But, very quickly, Che showed himself much less competent in politics than in military matters. First as President of the National Bank of Cuba, then as Minister for Industry, he proved to be clumsy and undiplomatic. Seven years later, Che and Castro had fallen out. For the Argentinian, the Revolution had become bureaucratized, and he abandoned his desk at the Ministry to take the field once again – a task for which destiny had singled him out. He left Cuba after writing a long letter to his friend Fidel, whom he no longer understood. From then on Che went from failure to failure, reiterating his suicidal battle-cry of 'Two, three, many Vietnams'. In the Congo, a shambolic and callous mob of revolutionaries were quick to abandon him. In Bolivia his campaign became bogged down, and he was taken prisoner. On 9 October 1967, some anonymous Bolivian NCO, after swallowing a large dose of aguardiente for courage, put an end to the legend.

But even in death, Che Guevara had a smile on his lips.

The ubiquitous Che. His portrait is usually reproduced from the famous Korda photo of 1967. Overleaf: Many artists exhibit their pictures near the cathedral.

same. Flat-swapping has been the subject of a hilarious film by one of the younger generation of Cuban directors.

CIGARS AND OTHER THINGS

The Prado ends at the Parque Central. Here the Cuban flag flutters in the centre of the square, as if to the dance music drifting over from the Café du Louvre on the Hotel Inglaterra's terrace. A marble statue of José Martí looks the other way. At the corner of the Inglaterra begins the Boulevard, once a street full of prestigious stores. This sector of Habana Vieja is the particular haunt of the *jinteros*, young hustlers or 'tourist-chasers' selling everything and nothing: cigars, rum, American cars … They are all agents for bigger fish, and the stuff on offer is rarely genuine. They often hang out near the Gran Teatro de la Habana, which is used by the National Opera, and also contains the Teatro García Lorca. The present Gran Teatro is a magnificent neo-baroque monument dating from 1838. Sarah Bernhardt once

*F*rom 1940 to 1958, thousands of Cubans bought their cars from the States. Hence the impressive number of American vehicles on the streets of Havana and in the provinces. In the capital alone there are reckoned to be some 100,000, with four times as many on the whole island.

Las Playas del Este, Havana's beaches, starting 18 kilometres (11 miles) from the capital, are nowadays run with tourism in mind.

played in this fairy-tale theatre. Today, the Camagüey ballet gives its marvellous performances there.

The determined walker will press on to the Capitol (Capitolio Nacional), similar to that in Washington, and constructed from 1929 to 1932. Its white dome, 62 metres (203 ft) high, is a good landmark for lost pedestrians. Until the Revolution, this was the home of the Senate and the House of Representatives. Today it houses the Cuban Academy of Sciences and the National Library of Science and Technology. Inside, there is a 17-metre (56 ft) statue of Jupiter, representing the state. The huge diamond in the entrance hall symbolizes the point from which all distances on the island are calculated. Hidden away behind this impressive monument – which you reach up an interminable flight of steps – lies Havana's small Chinatown. Just a few streets, a market, and excellent terrace restaurants. Not far from here, a sign announcing the Partagás tobacco company sways above the great doorways of one of the oldest

and most famous factories in Cuba. Going into it is like entering a sanctuary. Inside, an almost religious silence reigns. There is something very scholarly about the manufacture of cigars – perhaps that is the secret of producing a good Havana? All the same, the indescribable monotony of this conveyor belt system is palpable. On the wall, to encourage the workers at their tasks, are portraits of Che, Cienfuegos, and José Martí.

HABANA VIEJA

In the 1920s, Calle Obispo stood for everything that was chic, rare, and precious: there was no street like it in all the Antilles. But for the tropical heat you might have been in New York or Paris. The shops overflowed with pastries and other delicacies; there was fine lingerie from Europe, panama hats from Central America, suits from London and perfumes from Paris. The Drogería Johnson, still structurally intact, gives a slight idea of the shops of that era, built of marble and

The panoramic view from the start of the Malecón, which stretches for 5 kilometres (3 miles) as far as the residential quarter of Miramar. The waterfront of Old Havana, with the Capitolio in the background and, far right, the angels on the Opera House (Gran Teatro de la Habana).
Preceding pages:
Modern Havana seen from El Morro fortress.

rare woods. But, little by little, Calle Obispo is being restored – as is the whole of Habana Vieja in recent years.

Old Havana never entirely lost its beauty, but by 1990 the theme of grandeur and decline monopolized public debate, and there was unending nostalgia for the city's past glories ... Yet matters were already improving. The very first step was taken, in fact, in 1982, when Cuba was still not open to tourists: UNESCO decided to list the 142 hectares (351 acres) of Old Havana among its World Heritage Sites. Within five years, a score of monuments and important buildings had been renovated. In 1986 the man appeared on the scene who was to become the leading light of the colossal restoration campaign. He was Eusébio Leal, the city's official historian – backed by a whole team of architects, and students from Havana's art colleges. It was in the early 1990s, when the 'Green Crocodile Island' was gradually opened up to the dollar, that the restoration team set about the gigantic task of renovating not only the monuments but the hotels, restaurants, and

The Malecón at sunset. All the houses are due for renovation by the year 2000.

cafés as well. Today, more than sixty buildings are under reconstruction in Old Havana. One of the most impressive sites is the Plaza Vieja, where work is in progress on twenty or so eighteenth-century buildings, as well as the Hotel Viena, whose architecture is pure art nouveau. So, after many years of neglect, the historic heart of Havana is being reborn. Of course, the process is not without setbacks. Between the houses which have already been restored, others are falling into ruin. Stone crumbles from balconies, people are crowded into tiny rooms and, on the roofs, pigs and chickens search for food. This is the other side of the coin – the one the tourist never sees.

THE CATHEDRAL

The visitor exploring the city's pedestrian thoroughfares will automatically arrive at the most famous square in Old Havana: the Plaza de la Catedral. The cathedral gives the illusion of being built in

black and white. Constructed by the Jesuits in the eighteenth century, its style is an elegant baroque with undertones of Florence. Some years ago, it was re-opened for the 10.30 a.m. Sunday mass. The small street to the left of the cathedral leads to the Bodeguita del Medio, a famous bodega opened in 1942, which quickly became a literary watering-hole where you drank *mojitos* and dined cheaply on pork and beans. It was here, in fact, that the *mojito* – later to become the national drink – was invented. One version consists of 4½ centilitres (say one third of a gill) of white rum (Havana Club), a spoonful of sugar, the juice of half an unripe lemon, a few sprigs of mint, and three drops of Angostura, all topped up with soda water. Everyone, from the most famous to the utterly anonymous, has memories of this bar – just look at the mass of graffiti on the walls and the wooden tables. 'The Bodeguita has been round the world. Each one of its tables is a continent.' The chair on which Hemingway used to sit is suspended from the ceiling.

'*H*abanera' of mixed black and white race: the work of a young artist.

*This western province, some 178 kilometres (110 miles)
from Havana, is known simply as Indigo Land.
Put another way, the finest landscapes in Cuba.*

THE PROVINCE OF
Pinar del Río

*Set amidst the splendours of
nature, bohíos – thatched huts
occupied by peasants working on
the tobacco plantations near Viñales
– offer a modicum of comfort.*

A chain of mountains winds through Pinar del Río, following the curve of Cuba's westernmost tip. At intervals rise the Sierra de los Órganos, the Sierra del Rosario, and, further south, Las Lomas. Life here is rural: simple, but not impoverished. Time seems to pass more slowly, and it is a far cry from the hectic pace of the capital. The town of Pinar del Río itself is somewhat chaotic; its fine monuments, like the Palacio Guasch, dating from the start of the century, mingle with the jumble of modern apartment blocks, post-Stalinist constructions, and decaying colonial mansions.

But travel the 25-odd kilometres (16 miles) north of Pinar and everything changes. 'Room with a view' is as true here as ever it could be. From the balconies of the pink-and-blue Hotel Los Jazmines, visitors can spend hours contemplating the landscape of the Valle de Viñales, where the horizon is lined with small, sugar-loaf mountains covered with tufts of dark green vegetation. In the heart of the peaceful valleys, in the Jurassic era, karstic processes gave rise to these conical limestone monoliths known locally as *mogotes*, formations found nowhere else save in the southern Chinese region of Guilin – Chinese artists never tire of immortalizing them inpen-and-ink drawings.

Here, there are only the straw-hatted *vaqueros*, Cuban-style cowboys, who follow the endless, red dirt-trails on horseback. The landscape is dotted with farms and curing-shacks for the tobacco – triangular structures thatched with palm leaves to keep in the humidity and freshness. This region produces the best types of tobacco plant in the world. Waking up amid this scenery is a unique and magical experience: you can watch the flight of kites and herons, and sniff the morning air, which is as pure as that of the Andes. At the foot of the *mogotes*, the small, country sounds seem muted or lost in the vastness of the landscape. The little village of Viñales is typical: its one main street is lined with sun-drenched verandas where people bask in rocking-chairs. Along the snaking roads, women sell *guarapo*, a delicious juice made from sugar cane.

It is within the triangle of the Vuelta Abajo, amongst these luxuriant *vegas* (plantations), that the 40,000 hectares (160 sq miles) of 'tobacco-land' are to be found. The Indians called this strange plant

The tobacco growing region, around Viñales and Pinar del Río, covers 40,000 hectares (160 sq miles). The sunshine, temperature, and humidity make it an ideal site. The leaves are dried in shacks covered with palms – 'casas de tabaco'.

The 'torcedora' uses the 'copa', a very thin leaf, for the outer layer of the cigar. Various other leaves form the interior. The cigars are then made into small bundles and dried for a fortnight in warm rooms.

cohiba. They inhaled the smoke from the leaves through their noses. The *conquistadores* very quickly came to appreciate this was a drug with anaesthetic properties, and decided to grow tobacco as a commercial crop. They built plantation towns like San Luis, San Juan y Martínez, and Pinar del Río.

In its own way, the tobacco plant is just as fussy as the vine. It needs exactly the right amount of sunshine, humidity, and warmth – the magic formula found in these fairy-tale valleys. Furthermore, like wine, tobacco is a living thing; it detests variations in temperature and cannot stand harsh treatment. Planting is carried out from September to December, and the harvest is taken two to four months later. At this point, the plants can reach 1.5 metres in height – nearly 5 feet. Once cut, the leaves are set out to dry for four days in the open air, on hurdles, then in the *casas de tabaco* scattered all over the plains. The leaves are sorted according to their quality. Some will form the *copa* or outer layer of the cigar, others the next layer, the *hoja de combustión,*

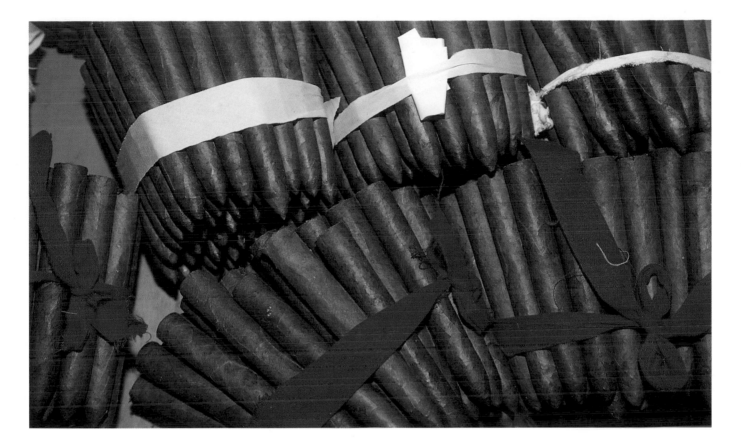

which causes the tobacco to burn evenly, or the *hoja de fortaleza*, for flavour. The final, innermost leaf is the *tripa*, which gives the cigar its shape. The famous *torcedoras*, women reputed to roll Havanas on their thighs, have skills which are passed on from one generation to the next; their art goes back as far as the eighteenth century. It takes nine months to train a good worker. The working day is eight hours long, during which time the *torcedores* make about 120 cigars. Che is said to have got through seven cigars a day, despite the fact that he suffered from asthma. When his doctors ordered him to cut down to one, the tobacco companies created a special monster cigar for him – *el immenso* – 58 centimetres (23 inches) long. Fidel Castro officially gave up smoking in 1985, after a vigorous anti-smoking campaign by the World Health Organization. The French refer to a good cigar as *un havane*; the Spanish call it *un puro*; the Cubans, *un tabaco*. '*Un tabaco* is like a beautiful girl. The *copa* is just her clothes: that is not important. What counts is what's underneath!'

In the cigar-factories, the tobacco leaves are first separated, then humidified, and dried again. The 'tripa' gives the cigar its shape, the 'hoja de fortaleza' its strength, the 'hoja de combustión' allows it to burn evenly, and the 'copa' is the outer wrapping. Before this last leaf is added, the cigar is pressed for thirty minutes to produce the right size.

From here, as in a road movie, you can embark on a long odyssey heading southwards in several stages till you reach the coast of Oriente.

THE MID-WEST

A mulatto woman; with lighter skin, she would be described as 'trigueña'.

CÁRDENAS

To leave Varadero is to plunge into the belly of the Green Crocodile. From here you can embark on a long odyssey heading southwards in several stages till you reach the coast of Oriente. Of course, the only way to travel is in a canary-yellow Chevrolet Bel Air!

The first place you come to is Cárdenas, which tends to be known as 'Buggyville', more by necessity than choice. Cárdenas is the epitome of all those sleepy little communities with nothing to offer but their peace and quiet. Like all Cuban towns, it revolves round a central square, in this case the Parque Colón, named after the bronze statue of Christopher Columbus (Cristóbal Colón) which dominates the surroundings. But this is not just any old statue; it is the oldest statue of the explorer in Cuba, probably in all South America, and is reckoned to have been cast in France. Facing Columbus stands a church. A remarkably large one – the Catedral de la Inmaculada Concepción. Opposite the church is an old hotel, the Dominica, dating from 1830. This is awfully colonial, but also *awfully* dilapidated. Cárdenas smells of sugar. Immediately outside the town, the landscape is engulfed by cane fields. On the road there is a continuous stream of cane-laden lorries and mechanical

harvesters. This scene is given the final touch by the flights of herons and the bare-chested cutters at work in the plantations. And across the sky drift the smoke-plumes from the sugar refineries.

THE HEROES OF SANTA CLARA

Just 70 kilometres (44 miles) from Cárdenas, in the very heart of agricultural land, stands Santa Clara, a living memorial of the guerillas' victory over the regulars of the dictator Batista. The famous battle of December 1958, which immortalized Che Guevara as a hero of the Revolution was fought here. The loyalist air force was bombarding the town. Che and his force fell back to the Santa Clara Hotel, where they received an incredible piece of news: an armoured munitions train was due to pass near the town, heading south. The decision to attack was immediate. And a handful of men, with Molotov cocktails and a bulldozer, managed to capture wagons designed to be impregnable. The announcement

of the *barbudos'* triumph was a grave blow to the morale of the government troops. What was more, the revolutionaries now had more than enough weapons. Three days after this feat, Santa Clara fell into the hands of the rebels, Batista was on his way out, and on 18 January 1959 Che and Camilo Cienfuegos made a victorious entry into Havana.

Santa Clara is proud of its glorious past. Though the hotel – rebaptized Santa Clara Libre (Free Santa Clara) – has been repainted green, they have kept the bullet-holes on the front wall. This hotel overlooks the Parque Vidal, which is the heart of the town. During recreation time at the secondary school nearby, the park is filled with white and yellow uniforms and the shrill cries of children. Not that this troubles the old men gossiping on their stone benches in the shade. On the other side of the Parque is the Teatro la Caridad, erected by a wealthy town family at the end of the last century. The Italian tenor Enrico Caruso once sang here.

Cárdenas, nicknamed 'Buggyville', has 75,000 inhabitants and is 20 kilometres (12½ miles) from Varadero. There is a peaceful atmosphere here, without throngs of tourists.

Just outside the town is an open-air museum commemorating the attack on the armoured train, with five of the original wagons on display. Inside these is a whole range of items used during the action. But today the most famous monument is the mausoleum of Che Guevara, which, since 17 October 1997, has contained the remains of the rebel leader, who met his end in Bolivia thirty years earlier. This mausoleum is situated off the Avenida de los Defiles to the west of the town, on a habitually deserted square renamed for the occasion Plaza de la Revolución Che Guevara. It is a place of sober contemplation. Fans of Che will wish to visit and admire the hero's relics inside the monument. The bronze statue, 7 metres (23 ft) high, is the work of the military sculptor Delarra, who flooded the schools with giant statues of Lenin, Marx, and Engels.

A flower-seller at Santa Clara, a city of 200,000 inhabitants, where Che won fame by attacking an armoured train.
A young 'blanca', out of school uniform. High-school girls in their uniform of white blouses and yellow skirts.

*T*he statue of Che dominating the Plaza de la Revolución was erected in 1987
to mark the twentieth anniversary of the guerilla leader's death.
In 1997 the site became a mausoleum where Che's remains were interred.

• Revolution or death! •

Things had started badly. The attack on the Moncada Barracks, in July 1953, was a disaster, and Fidel was sentenced to fifteen years' hard labour. Two years later, Batista granted him amnesty. Castro then spent a whole year organizing an attempt to invade Cuba from Mexico, using the motor-vessel Granma. Again, he failed. A handful of the rebels escaped and took to the mountains of the Sierra Maestra. The ensuing guerilla campaign was to last for more than two years till, finally, 300 revolutionaries got the better of the 12,000 demoralized loyalist troops. On the evening of 1 January 1959, Batista fled to Santo Domingo. Fidel and his men seized Havana, and the Revolution was born. What began as a kind of Utopian socialism gradually drifted towards hard-line communism, with the backing of the Soviet Union.

On the statue's base is carved one of the Revolution's famous slogans: *Hasta la victoria siempre*. Ever Onwards to Victory! Lower down there is a copy of the letter Che sent to Fidel when he decided to quit Cuba. You can also read quotes from Che's political philosophy, such as: 'Voluntary work is the school which teaches conscience.'

Moving on from Santa Clara towards the Atlantic, you reach Remedios, a town of 20,000 people, and off the traditional tourist track. But in the direction of the Caribbean lies Cienfuegos, which is both an industrial centre and a coastal resort.

THE DISCREET CHARM OF THE PROVINCES

The third largest city in Cuba, Cienfuegos, has plenty of charm. It is hard to tell exactly why. Maybe it is because the city, situated at the curve of a great bay, is broad and airy, with the Paseo del Prado running right through the centre and developing into a seafront (the Malecón) lined with 1950s-style houses. Maybe also because it always seems full of life, like its pedestrian thoroughfare, the Avenida San Fernando. This street is bordered with colonnades and dozens of little shops selling everything and anything. It is the haunt of young, short-skirted girls, many of French origin – particularly from Bordeaux. In fact, in the early nineteenth century, José Cienfuegos, the governor, wanted to 'change the colour of the town', being of the opinion that it was over-crowded with Negroes. He asked a Frenchman, Luis de Clouet, to encourage a number of his compatriots to come and settle in Cienfuegos, which was finally rebuilt in 1831 after a violent cyclone. This is why many French people, from Bordeaux and Louisiana, decided to migrate to Cienfuegos. Is this also the reason why they say Cienfuegos's

The Teatro Tomás Terry stands on the Parque José Martí. Cienfuegos is delightfully reminiscent of Paris, and is twinned with Bordeaux.
Overleaf:
Colonial houses on the Malecón at Cienfuegos. These fine buildings were once the homes of French settlers.

The colonial charm of Cienfuegos, which is also Cuba's most industrialized city. Nicknamed the 'Pearl of the South', it has a population of 125,000.

women are the finest on the Island? At the entrance to the bay, the Castillo de Jagua, built by the Spanish, has been watching over the city since 1745. The fishing village of Perché huddles at its foot.

But back to the Parque José Martí. On Saturday mornings, the bandstand is vibrant with *salsa* music. The cathedral occupies one side of the park, whilst on the other the Teatro Tomás Terry, with its baroque façade, hosts ballet troupes and folklore companies. Cienfuegos has always been proud of its cultural achievements. This boast is borne out by the Casa de la Cultura Benjamin Duarte in the Palacio de Ferrer, the Galería de Arte Universal, and the Museo Histórico, where you can see a complete collection of household furniture used by French families in the last century.

The Prado ends in the district of Punta Gorda, once the up-market quarter occupied by the American Mafia. American cars from the 1940s are parked outside villas of the same era – astonished visitors must feel someone has waved a magic wand and turned the clock

back. At the far end of the town is the large Hotel Jagua, once a casino famous throughout Cuba, and owned by Batista's son. Opposite stands the imposing Palacio de Valle built in a medley of styles – neo-classical, Gothic, Moorish and Byzantine. Today, transformed into a restaurant, it is a delightful place to listen to the pianist playing yesterday's hits whilst you enjoy a dish of Cuban lobster. About 18 kilometres (11 miles) south of Cienfuegos is the sweeping beach of Rancho Luna, the city's rather neglected watering-place. Then visit the Jardín Botánico Soledad – the oldest botanical gardens on the island, and the finest in Latin America according to the experts – containing some 2,000 species, including 280 kinds of palm and 69 species of orchid. Further south still, you enter the Sierra del Escambray mountains, where the man-made Hanabanilla lake lies secluded amidst lovely mountain scenery. This is a paradise for fishermen, and the big hotel overlooking the lake offers Turkish baths and a heated swimming pool!

Neo-classical and baroque rub shoulders in the city of Cienfuegos. Above is the Palacio de Valle, erected in 1917. Batista intended to make it a casino; today it is a famous restaurant.

Trinidad always appeared to be
enjoying an eternal siesta.
At least, for a whole century ...

TRINIDAD,
home of Fine Arts

Only the bell tower remains of the former eighteenth-century convent of St Francis of Assisi. The site is now used as a national museum for the Lucha Contra Bandidos (Struggle against the Bandits); the counter-revolutionaries who hid themselves in the Sierra del Escambray between 1960 and 1965.

This was once a peaceful *pueblo*, dozing in the oppressive heat, living life at the slow pace of the horse-drawn vehicles that rattled over the uneven cobblestones of its narrow streets. Then, all of a sudden, one morning in 1991, the first coach disgorged its hordes of camera-wielding trippers in their shorts and baseball caps. Since then, it has never stopped. But Trinidad, founded in 1514 by Diego Velázquez, has managed to retain both its calm and its attractiveness. Philosophically, the locals let the morning tourist storm roll over them, and only begin their activities later on, around five in the evening. Then the sun has set, the shadows are lengthening, and the streets gradually fill with people going casually about their business. But it must be said too that this has brought an unexpected influx of tourists whose money has breathed new life into the economy of a town that desperately needed it.

Trinidad is well aware of this. It is listed as the most beautiful town in Cuba. All the tourist guides, all the books, all the historians have said so and are still saying so. In particular, it is the best preserved, the most intact of the seven original towns founded by the first *conquistadores*. Why should this be so? The reason is that Trinidad fell back into a blissful sort of lethargy after two centuries of great

prosperity – the seventeenth and the eighteenth. These were the town's glory days, with everything depending on sugar cane. The wealthy planters had their homes in this small town with its protective circle of mountains, and it lay close to their plantations. Rich businessmen followed in their turn, and the slave-traders made a fortune. In the nineteenth century, cane sugar was replaced by beet, which was much cheaper. Trinidad's brilliance was eclipsed. The wealthy departed to make money elsewhere, leaving their mansions just as they were. So, drifting back into oblivion, the town became frozen in time. Even the War of Independence hardly affected it: the clocks seem to have stopped for ever in the 1700s. Today this is a benefit which can be enjoyed by visitors, and, since 1989, Trinidad has been listed as a World Heritage Site by UNESCO. From the tower of the Museo de Arqueología Guamuhaya, whose top is reached up a narrow, winding stairway, there is a view stretching over the entire historic district. At its centre lies the

The Museo Romántico, an old mansion of a dozen or so rooms where the town's entire colonial past is retraced in displays of furniture and everyday objects. A marble statue on Trinidad's Plaza Mayor.

Trinidad (50,000 inhabitants) has retained its cobbled streets, its tiled roofs, and its fine wrought-iron window grilles. It is regarded as a museum town.

spreading Plaza Mayor, a pretty square shaded by palm trees and surrounded by large private houses and bougainvilleas. Children crawl excitedly over the stone dogs guarding the entrances. The building housing the Museo, made entirely of wood, is regularly used by Cuban and foreign companies as a set for historical films. The parish church opposite (Iglesia Parroquial de la Santísima Trinidad) is only open at certain times. On its left stands the mansion formerly owned by the Counts of Brunet, now known as the Museo Romántico. Its thirteen rooms re-create all the happy, prosperous atmosphere of a wealthy nineteenth-century home. From one of its balconies, you can see the façade of the church which once formed part of the Convent of St Francis of Assisi. In the adjacent streets, women work at their embroidery behind the wooden bars of their houses, and men rock themselves in chairs worn out by decades of siestas. At the Canchánchara, a patio-bar set amidst plants and trees, the cigar-smoke rises to a background of

rumba music improvised by a band fortified with the house special. This is a mixture of rum, lemon, honey, and water. The rumba derives from a mixture of African rhythms and the Spanish *décima*. Other Cuban music includes the traditional *danzón* – descendant of a French *contredanse* from Haiti, and from which developed the mambo – and the Creole-based *son*, originating in Oriente. The word salsa indicates a type of hybrid Latin music: son, rumba, mambo, cha-cha-chá, and jazz.

Suddenly, as you turn the corner of what seems like any ordinary street, you come across a wide porch. Go through this and you find an elegant shop, dating from a bygone era. Amid the 1900-style *décor*, you can look at yourself in a mirror made in 1850 or thumb through historical archives laid out on period furniture. Above your head hangs a big, crystal chandelier. You cannot buy anything: only look and touch. This is typical Cuba. Heritage is not for sale. Though Trinidad is often referred to as a museum town, it does not

Street scene in Trinidad.
Opposite: Numerous 'paladares' have opened in this tourist centre. The word 'paladar' basically means 'palate'. 'Paladares' are 'private' restaurants allowed a maximum of twelve places; you eat in the owners' houses.
Overleaf:
On the right, the parish church of Trinidad, with, further on, the Museo Romántico and the bell tower of San Francisco de Asís.

*M*any craftsmen have set
themselves up in Trinidad's
tourist-packed streets.
Embroidery is one of the
region's specialities.

come across as a series of lifeless exhibits. This 'museum' is a living one: it is everywhere. You have only to peep into the houses to realize this. The owners will be pleased to show off everything of beauty the town contains. The Casa Mauri, behind the Plaza Mayor, has a giant stuffed crocodile on the table. There you can rent a room in colonial Louis XV style. The Casa Estrella María de Sayas goes back to the middle of the nineteenth century. All the furniture is from that period, in mahogany. The ceilings are 9 metres (nearly 30 ft) high, keeping the rooms continually airy. The Casa Munoz, which belonged to an old family originating in Italy and Catalonia whose lands were confiscated during the Revolution, has gasoliers, a Louis XV bed with gold-banded posts, and floor-tiling from the end of the last century. Obviously, the streets of Trinidad are hiding some real treasures. These are tucked away behind ordinary-looking house-fronts and french windows whose ornately turned wooden frames betray the ravages of time.

Inside the Museo Romántico are exhibits of furniture from France, Austria, Spain, and of course, from the Antilles. Cane rocking-chair from the Museo in a typical blend of Spanish and Cuban styles.

The Museo de Arquitectura Colonial, housed in a magnificent mansion dating from 1738 and redesigned early last century. Courtyard of a typical colonial guest-house in Trinidad. This is the Casa Mauri, 254 years old. The family, Catalonian in origin, were tobacco planters.

It was the Valle de los Ingenios (Valley of the Sugar Mills), lying between Trinidad and Sancti Spíritus, which made the fortune of both Trinidad and the cane-planters. Already, at the end of the sixteenth century, Cuba was being talked of as the world's sugar reserve. In 1837, railways came to the island, even before they reached Spain, and sugar production soared. Some eighty sugar mills were working flat out in the valley, now listed as a World Heritage Site. The magnificence of the Manaca Iznaga plantation house with its 43.5-metre (143 ft) lookout-tower gives an idea of the wealth of the original owners; the tower was used to keep an eye on the *macheteros* (cane-cutters). After the Revolution, the *machetero* armed with his *machete* symbolised freedom and the struggle against exploitation and slavery. Finally, even one of the landowners, Carlos Manuel de Céspedes, revolted by the living conditions of the slaves, armed his *macheteros*. With the battle-cry of *Cuba Libre* – Free Cuba – they hurled themselves against the Spanish regulars.

The Torre Iznaga, on the sugar planation of the same name, was both a symbol of the owners' wealth and a means of overseeing the slaves at work. The plantation-house (Manaca Iznaga) is now a restaurant.

The Valle de los Ingenios (Valley of the Sugar Mills), which begins 8 kilometres (5 miles) from Trinidad, is a fertile area, thick with sugar cane. Sugar made the fortunes of the eighteenth- and nineteenth-century planters. Till the middle of the last century, the valley had some eighty mills. Since 1989, it has been listed as a World Heritage Site.

*Rum, soul-mate of salsa music, just had to be Cuban,
and is inextricably linked to the island's mythology.*

• Rum cocktails •

'No rum without music, no music without rum.' So said Fernando Campoamor, author of a rum-drinkers' 'bible' entitled Happy Son of Sugar Cane. Rum, soul-mate of salsa music, just had to be Cuban, and is inextricably linked to the island's mythology. Yesterday Havana Club, today Barcardí. Hemingway, an incurable alcoholic, drank his *mojitos* at the Bodeguita and his daiquiris at the Floridita. These were the bars – frequented by North-American high rollers – where the two legendary *cocteles*, both based on rum, were invented by barmen (*cantineros*) as talented as they were worldly wise. It was at the end of the nineteenth century that Cuban rum really acquired an international reputation. Then it ousted Spanish brandy and French cognac. It received, in fact, the ultimate accolade – it was served at the Moulin Rouge.

*Three small towns form a triangle
in the middle of the island –
Sancti Spíritus, Ciego de Ávila, and Morón.*

The colonial
TOWNS

Ciego de Ávila, now with 85,000 inhabitants, was founded in the 1840s and boasts little colonial architecture. This door is an exception.

Three small towns form a triangle in the very heart of the island. These are Sancti Spíritus, Ciego de Ávila, and Morón. The first, and the only truly colonial town, is a sort of miniature Trinidad, but without the tourists. In fact, few people go there. It is none the less one of the seven original towns founded by the Spanish at the start of the Conquest. The Iglesia Parroquial Mayor del Espíritu Santo was first built of wood in 1522; not surprisingly, it was soon destroyed by pirates, and the present stone structure dates from 1680. Ciego de Ávila, the provincial capital, has a less dramatic history than Sancti Spíritus, but boasts immense pineapple plantations. But what of Morón, whose emblem is a cockerel? (The statue of a rearing fighting-cock can be seen at the entrance to the town.) Well, it is a rather likeable place which the rest of Cuba regards as the 'fiesta capital' of the island. It is nearer the truth to say that the people are blessed with a naturally happy disposition. Here are no really large places in which to stage celebrations, with the possible exceptions of the small central square and Rooster Park. Still, in the evening, the townspeople bring rocking-chairs, bottles of rum, and transistors out into the streets – which livens up the place no end. But Morón is also an inevitable staging-post on the way to Cayo Coco and Cayo Guillermo, two small islands of the Archipiélago de

Situated between Santa Clara and Camagüey, Ciego de Ávila lies on the 'carretara' (main road) leading south. The town has an impressive number of arcaded streets.

Camagüey. This lies off the Atlantic coast – but can be reached by land! There is a 27-kilometre (17-mile) causeway between the mainland and Cayo Coco, and another, 17 kilometres (around 11 miles) long, joining this island with Cayo Guillermo. These causeways resemble the links between some of the Keys beyond the Straits of Florida. Along these roads you meet nothing except birds – rosy flamingoes and ibises in particular. The Cayos are uninhabited except by tourists and hotel staff, and the hotels are very much like those in big American resorts.

CAMAGÜEY: A FINE CITY

To all intents and purposes, the South begins here. Cubans tell you this is not the real beginning of Oriente, but there is that atmosphere, that curious feel of the South. You first notice it in the city's road system: twisting and twining, streets set off in every direction, an absolute maze of narrow thoroughfares and cul-de-sacs, and a nightmare for drivers. Rumour has it that the convoluted layout was dreamt up to

make things harder for raiders after the English pirate Henry Morgan

sacked the city in 1668. The result is this impenetrable tangle. Some

streets still have their old tramlines, others are littered with arrow signs

as if for a treasure-hunt. There is a labyrinthine one-way system, and

the traffic reminds you of some Asian city, with the rickshaw-like

bicitaxis racing each other amidst a cacophony of bells and hooters.

Camagüey's streets are a constant source of discoveries. Plunge into

them and lose yourself. Stroll by the vast hairdressing salons with their

green, reclining seats, past La Gran Antilla where weary salesgirls await

the unlikely arrival of customers for ancient stocks of clothes from

heaven knows where in the old Soviet bloc. Push open the glass doors

of the Gran Hotel; take a peep at its faded opulence; sit on one of its

big red velvet armchairs. Then make your way into the courtyard of a

colonial house to admire the wonderful *tinajones* – wide terracotta

pots typical of the city. In the sixteenth century, Catalonian potters

brought their skills with them and developed the craft here. Nowadays mere decorative objects, these pots were formerly used to keep rainwater fresh, or to preserve either oil or grain. Some are as much as 4 metres (13 ft) in circumference. Every Saturday evening, Calle República, Camagüey's main thoroughfare, is closed to traffic. Snack-bars are set up on the pavements, everyone eats spareribs, plays music, and dances in the middle of the street.

A PLACE OF PROSPERITY

A colonial city in the true sense, Camagüey was founded by Diego Velázquez in 1514, but by no means on its present site. The original village was by the sea, in the Bay of Nuevitas. However, weary of endless pirate raids, its inhabitants moved inland, to a new site near two rivers. This was an Indian territory, from which the city takes its name. In due course it turned its attention to stock-rearing and sugar cane. Camagüey has always been prosperous; today the nearby plains provide grazing for Cuba's largest dairy herds. The city had its own hero in the First War of Independence against the Spanish – Ignacio Agramonte. A museum has been opened in the house where he was born, giving a good idea of life amongst well-off families in the first half of the nineteenth century. He died at the age of 32 after fifty or so battles. The Parque Agramonte is one of the prettiest *plazas* in Camagüey, with its little green benches, its vast, triple-naved cathedral, and its Casa de la Trova (literally, Ballad House), where the best musicians in town come to play in the delightful courtyard garden. This square is the city's nerve-centre. This is where you arrange to meet people, and the departure-point for the adjoining streets and other *plazas*, such as Los Trabajadores and San Juan de Dios. The latter is the perfect example of an eighteenth-century *plaza*, flanked by a church from the early 1700s and an old hospital founded in 1728. An added

Camagüey (population: 300,000) is the most colonial of Cuba's cities – after Trinidad. Its streets are tortuous and confusing.
Overleaf:
Preparation of theatrical scenery. The Camagüey ballet company is famous throughout the country. Many cultural events and exhibitions of art and pottery take place in the city.

bonus is the pleasant restaurant sited in a colonial house called La Campana de Toledo. You can also visit the birthplace of another of Camagüey's famous sons, Nicolás Guillén; the house was only opened to the public in 1992. Guillén was considered the poet laureate of the entire Castro Revolution.

For the beaches nearest Camagüey, you will need to travel 80 kilometres or so (around 50 miles) to the south and Santa Cruz del Sur, or much further north to Santa Lucía where there are some of Cuba's best beaches, with 20-odd kilometres (some 12 miles) of white sand. As yet, the place has not really been developed, which is the source of its charm. Beside the four traditional hotels at intervals along the beach, *cabañas* (fishermen's cabins) can be hired for sleeping.

HAPPY-GO-LUCKY HOLGUÍN

Heading further towards Oriente, after crossing the province of Las Tunas, you arrive in a town founded for once not by Diego Velázquez

A wedding in Camagüey's City Hall. Couples rent their costumes for the occasion. People marry young in Cuba, usually before the age of 20. A girl may marry at 16, sometimes earlier with her parents' consent.
Opposite:
Typical interior of a small house in Camagüey. Throughout Cuba you can visit houses and talk to the owners. The welcome will be simple but warm.

*H*olguín's Iglesia de San José, on
one of the three squares forming the
town's centre. This is the quietest,
left mainly to children.

but by García Holguín, in 1525. He simply named it after himself. The town's layout is straightforward. The central area is designed around three *parques* forming a small arc. There are horse-drawn buggies, cycle-taxis looking like wheelchairs – they take one passenger each – lots of pedal bikes, and rocking-chairs in front of doorways. On the walls, slogans exhort less enthusiastic citizens not to forget the Revolution: *Holguineros, ¡al combate!* and *Batallando siempre…*

On the Parque Flore you can go and eat an ice-cream at the Cremería Guamá – if the queue is not too long. The Moorish façade of the Catedral de San Isidoro peers down over the trees. In the much quieter square in front of the Iglesia de San José it is the turn of a bronze angel to watch passers-by. The liveliest of all the *plazas*, especially in the evening, is the Calixto García, named after a hero of both wars of independence; he at one time commanded the eastern armies. There is a museum devoted to him in the house where he was born: the Casa Natal de Calixto García. The rest of the town's history can be studied

in the Museo de Historia Provincial. The most interesting features, however, remain the colonial façades scattered around the square, sometimes belonging to ordinary shops, sometimes a cinema, or a marble-floored Casa de la Trova under the arcades. A notice outside a ground-floor flat opening onto the street proclaims *Se cuidan bici*: 'Bikes looked after here'. Not far away, in a courtyard, a group of old men sitting on chairs are listening to *son*, popular Cuban music of Creole origin. This, then, is life at Holguín – laid back, happy-go-lucky. In the evenings, everyone arranges to meet friends in the squares. Music drifts down from the disco on the first floor of a large modern building. Those bars with air-conditioning – like fridges inside – are filling up with tourists; small groups of locals start impromptu dance-sessions around blaring radio cassettes. *Holguineros* are indeed a type of nocturnal animal.

In the eighteenth century a cross was set up on this hill overlooking Holguín, known as La Loma de la Cruz. It is reached up a flight of some 460 steps. Entertainment for old people in a courtyard off the Plaza de Calixto García.

CUBA'S FIRST INHABITANTS

Some 20 kilometres (12½ miles) from Holguín, on the Atlantic coast, a small dirt road leads to the Bay of Bariay, where Christopher Columbus first landed on the island on 28 October 1492. His exclamations of wonder are well known. Before him stretched a vista of emerald green. Thousands of birds were singing, and the natives welcomed the caravels like gods risen from the sea. The explorer thought he had reached the realms of the Great Khan. No one at the time knew that a vast continent, a whole New World, barred the way to the Indies. This was not the Cipango described in such glowing terms by Marco Polo, and supposedly all a-glitter with gold. None the less, this land was an Eden of its own. It was Cuba. Terracotta totems now watch over this place with its supernatural associations; it retains its romantic aura, even if re-creation has been somewhat overdone. The site is battered by the winds and echoes to the cries of the birds, just as it did 500 years ago.

Further along the coastline, towards the east, is Guardalavaca, the chief seaside resort of Oriente. It claims to have the best beaches in the South, and compares itself with Varadero. It has a long way to go. The resort is a tourist complex specializing in package holidays – there is little of the real atmosphere of Cuba, and no seaside village as such. A drive of ten minutes or so brings you to Chorro de Maita, where there is a museum in the form of a reconstructed Indian burial site. Traditionally the Taínos were buried in a foetal position; maybe their beliefs demanded they leave the world in the same way as they entered it. This was an achaeological discovery of immense significance, since some authorities believe these are the remains of Taínos from 10,000 years before Christ. In the small town of Banes, the centre for relevant research, is the Museo Indocubano, whose exhibition of the art, culture, and artefacts of the aboriginal peoples is one of the finest in all Cuba.

Holguín's 'bicitaxis' resemble pedal-rickshaws, and carry one passenger. 'Bicitaxis', as small-business ventures, date only from the last few years, when tourists returned in large numbers. Each town has different sorts of vehicles. Individuals decorate them to their taste, but they are state property.
Opposite:
The fourth largest city on the island, Holguín has a population of 225,000. Situated on the edge of Oriente, and not far from the beaches of Guardalavaca, it is becoming an important stopping-off place for tourists doing the rounds of southern Cuba.

Baracoa has all the elegance of a grand old lady who has fallen on hard times, but has not lost her style.

BARACOA:
the world's end

A lively group of schoolchildren; primary pupils wear red and white uniforms.
Opposite:
The little port of Baracoa, the first town to be founded by the Spanish. In the distance is El Yunque – The Anvil – a huge, flat mountain, which served as a landmark for sailors. Organized climbs are available.
Overleaf:
Baracoa (population: 50,000) has the usual charm of remote little ports in the Antilles. French colonists expelled from Haiti made it their first place of refuge. The town is sited on a promontory between two bays; all around there is tropical forest, where some descendants of the Taíno Indians are still living.

The first capital of the island was founded in 1512 by Diego Velázquez: he called it Nuestra Señora de la Asunción. Today it goes once more under its Indian name of Baracoa. It has all the charm of a bygone age, a nostalgia for the 'good old days', and that fading elegance of a colony whose past is beyond reproach. Very much, in fact, like the town's legendary figure, an astonishing woman known as *La Rusa*. After fleeing the communists and abandoning Holy Russia, she ended up in this remote little port in the Antilles, supporting the *barbudos* in the cause of that same communist ideology.

Magdalena Rovieskuya – Mimá to the locals – landed at Baracoa in the 1930s. She was an artist, a woman of great beauty, who spoke five languages, played the piano, and sang arias from the operas. She opened a private hotel, also called La Rusa, on the Malecón (promenade). The walls had the faded colours of Italian house-fronts, and, in her establishment, with its aura of a turn-of-the-century salon, Mimá received the polite society of Baracoa. Fidel Castro and Che spent time there. She died in 1978, and her adopted son, himself a painter, opened a museum in his own house, at 3 Ciro Froa, 50 metres (50-odd yards) from the hotel. This retraces the entire life of this warm-hearted and enterprising émigrée whose destiny, despite herself, was linked to that of the Revolution. The old lady's photographs and personal possessions

*M*any artists have taken up
residence in the town: the Baracoa
school is reckoned to be one of
Cuba's best.

jostle for space in a pleasantly chaotic collection. The hotel was reopened in 1993, renovated, and painted a rather garish yellow. Still, it does mean it can be seen from miles around!

Despite the systematic massacre of the Indians by the Spanish, some of the Taínos who occupied this former aboriginal stronghold managed to survive. The descendants of these proud and peace-loving people, Cuba's first inhabitants, are scattered amongst the surrounding mountains. The main square of Baracoa, the Plaza Cacique Hatuey, with its monument to the memory of the Taíno chieftain, is the nerve-centre of what is an overgrown coastal village. Chief Hatuey went to his death at the stake screaming defiance at the Christians. Later, in the eighteenth century, the Spanish built a fort at each end of the town to protect it against incessant attacks by pirates. A third fort, Seboruco, on the hill overlooking the town, has been made into a hotel.

The present church adjoining the Plaza Hatuey, Nuestra Señora de la Asunción, dates from 1805. Of the original building – made of wood

and palm-leaves – nothing now remains, save an important relic, the Cruz de la Parra, a cross which Christopher Columbus is said to have planted on landing in the bay. The sacristan of the church – he began as its verger at the age of 12 – receives visitors, and makes a great show of opening the glass door of the safe containing the cross. No one is permitted to take it out save the Pope – on his recent visit to Cuba, John Paul II, in his eagerness to touch it, had it brought to Santiago.

It is a pleasure to stroll around Baracoa and find a small, forgotten Caribbean port still intact. There are cobbled streets, rows of wooden, houses, horse-buggies and the sound of hoofs, stalls under the arcades, keen breezes blowing off the sea, children playing *pelota* (baseball) in the streets, the old-fashioned windows of a big store with a model of the *Granma* and the slogan: *¡Sigamos el verde oliva!* – Let's follow the Olive-Green! – a reference to the combat fatigues worn by the *barbudos*. Peace and goodwill reign in Baracoa, the town at the world's end, which was isolated from the rest of the island for over 450 years.

Classroom in a Baracoa school. For 450 years, the town was only accessible by sea. The road which now leads from Santiago to Baracoa was not built till the 1960s. A happy atmosphere reigns in this salon at the world's end.

Proud, artistic, a curious mixture,
the capital of Oriente has always
paraded its title of Cradle of the Revolution.

SANTIAGO,
rebel of the south

The Basílica del Cobre, near Santiago, is Cuba's most sacred pilgrimage site. People come from far and wide to pray to Cuba's patron, Nuestra Señora de la Caridad del Cobre. The present shrine dates from 1927.

The first thing to do on arriving in Santiago is to make straight for the heart of the city – the Parque Céspedes. Go up the steps of the Casa Granda Hotel, sit down at a table on the terrace, order a *mojito*, light up a *Lancero de Cohiba* – and start looking around you. Whatever the time of day, life is beautiful. A band is playing 'Comandante Che Guevara'. The sun is pouring down from above the buildings opposite. On your left you can see the outline of the cathedral, where a fine angel with a trumpet stands on the roof. From here, Santiago feels a bit like a spa town – an uneasy compromise, and somewhat noisy. In the Parque Céspedes, young and old come and sit on the benches in the public gardens, chatting away and calling out to foreigners, who pass on disdainfully. There is a constant procession of old American cars round the big square. Nothing is missing from the peaceful centre of this large provincial community, Cuba's second city, far from Havana (970 kilometres: 606 miles), and not a bit jealous. Proud, artistic, a curious mixture, the capital of Oriente has always paraded its title of 'Cradle of the Revolution'. The city was Fidel Castro's choice for his very first move against Batista's forces – the assault on the Moncada Barracks. The walls of the garrison still sport bullet-holes, and one wing has been transformed into a museum devoted to the exploits of 26 July 1953. On

the other side of the Casa Granda, the Casa de Velázquez, built at the start of the Spanish Conquest for the personal use of Diego Velázquez, is a perfect example of the Andalusian–South American house. It is a real jewel of colonial architecture, and classed as the oldest dwelling in Latin America. Inside, its rooms are dark and cool, the furniture plush and opulent, and its ebony *moucharabieh* (grilled shutters) is a pure masterpiece. Hernán Cortés stayed here before setting out to conquer Mexico. The vast City Hall, with its neo-classical façade, occupies the final side of this splendid *plaza*. Small, busy streets disappear in all directions to link up with other squares, such as the Plaza de Dolores, which is surrounded by bars and restaurants. Hordes of schoolchildren in uniform rush down the frighteningly steep steps connecting one street with another. Calle Enramada, the main shopping thoroughfare, has preserved the old signs of what, before the Revolution, were famous stores – El Louvre, La California, La Francia. Today their windows are full of junk. Not far off, impressed visitors stop to stare at the enormous

With its population of 420,000, Santiago is the second largest city in Cuba and considered an alternative capital.
Opposite:
The Parque Céspedes and its cathedral, Nuestra Señora de la Asunción. This is the heart of the city – a Spanish-style park, typical of the colonial period. At some time during the day, every santiaguero will pass through here. On the left, the Parque is overlooked by the terraces of the Casa Granda Hotel.

Santiago's streets are like those in all Cuban towns – people work, play, and live there. The French settlers of the nineteenth century made a great contribution to the cultural enrichment of a city which developed under Spanish and African influences.
Overleaf:
View over Santiago – the cathedral, the upper storeys of the Casa Granda (the white building), and, in the distance, the port. Inner Santiago has few 'high-rises' or the equivalent of council flats, the construction of cheap accommodation being confined to the outskirts.

Museo Emilio Bacardí. Behind its massive doors are spacious rooms devoted to aboriginal culture, the Spanish Conquest, and the wars of independence. There is even an Egyptian mummy on display.

Descending towards the modern city, you pass through the district of Sueño (Dreamland) with its gridded streets lined with coral trees and pretty, 1950s-style villas. Here, your attention is commanded by a giant, garish cube – the Santiago Hotel. This was the work of Santiago's Futurist School, giving pride of place to steel, tubular structures, and colour. The railway station is from the same stable, as is the Teatro Heredia, opposite the Plaza de la Revolución; this last is dedicated to Antonio Maceo, hero of the Second War of Independence, who died in battle in 1895. His statue shows him on horseback and surrounded by machetes, symbols of revolt. The Soviet-style realism is highly effective.

Beyond the Santiago Hotel begins the quarter known as Vista Alegre. Its grand neo-colonial houses enjoy cool gardens and the shade of spreading trees. 'The House', a replica of the one at Havana and offering the same facilities, is one of the crowning glories of this handsome, prosperous area, which has something of France about it. The fact is that there used to be a strong French presence in Santiago: colonists fleeing the revolt in Haiti all landed either at Baracoa or Santiago. They became coffee planters, and passed on some of their French culture to the town. Even now people dance the *rumba francesa*, a highly rhythmical form of minuet, invented by Haitian slaves working for the French.

Some 20 kilometres (12–13 miles) from Santiago is the town of El Cobre, which owes its name to the copper mines exploited by the Spanish; they soon exhausted the gold deposits and turned to copper instead. Nowadays, no one comes to El Cobre for copper, but there is a stream of pilgrims to the Basílica de la Virgen de la Caridad del Cobre. Even as you approach the shrine, roadside touts attempt to sell you

Monument to Antonio Maceo, hero of the 1895 war. The red beret is not necessarily a sign of membership of the CDR – Committee for the Defence of the Revolution. None the less, Santiago, the 'Cradle of the Revolution', is considered more communist than other communities.
Opposite:
A rare portrait of Fidel Castro. He has never been keen to be painted or photographed.

*T*he apartment of a santera, a priestess of the santería religion. The dolls represent divinities (orishas); like Christian saints, they each have their own function, and prayers are addressed to one or the other depending on the circumstances. This small altar is dedicated to St Lazarus, protector of the sick. It includes offerings of bread and flowers. Anyone invoking the saint's intercession must add a few dollars on entering and leaving the house.

• *Santería*: the religion of all the saints •

Santería is not some Cuban form of voodoo. It is a completely different form of religion, quite happily embracing Christian and pagan deities and beliefs both sacred and profane. A santera's house is open to all. People go there to get help in resolving a problem – usually something to do with health. In this Afro-Cuban religion, there are countless 'saints'. It is known, in fact, as the 'religion of all the saints' (*orishas*). Small altars, in each corner of the room, stand awaiting offerings; this is the price of the *orisha*'s intercession. Each family has its altar and its own *orisha*. It is estimated that seventy per cent of Cubans believe in *santería* and observe its rites, which consist of dances and trance-like states. Nothing is written down in *santería*. All is secret. The white robes symbolize purity; the turban stands for rebirth.

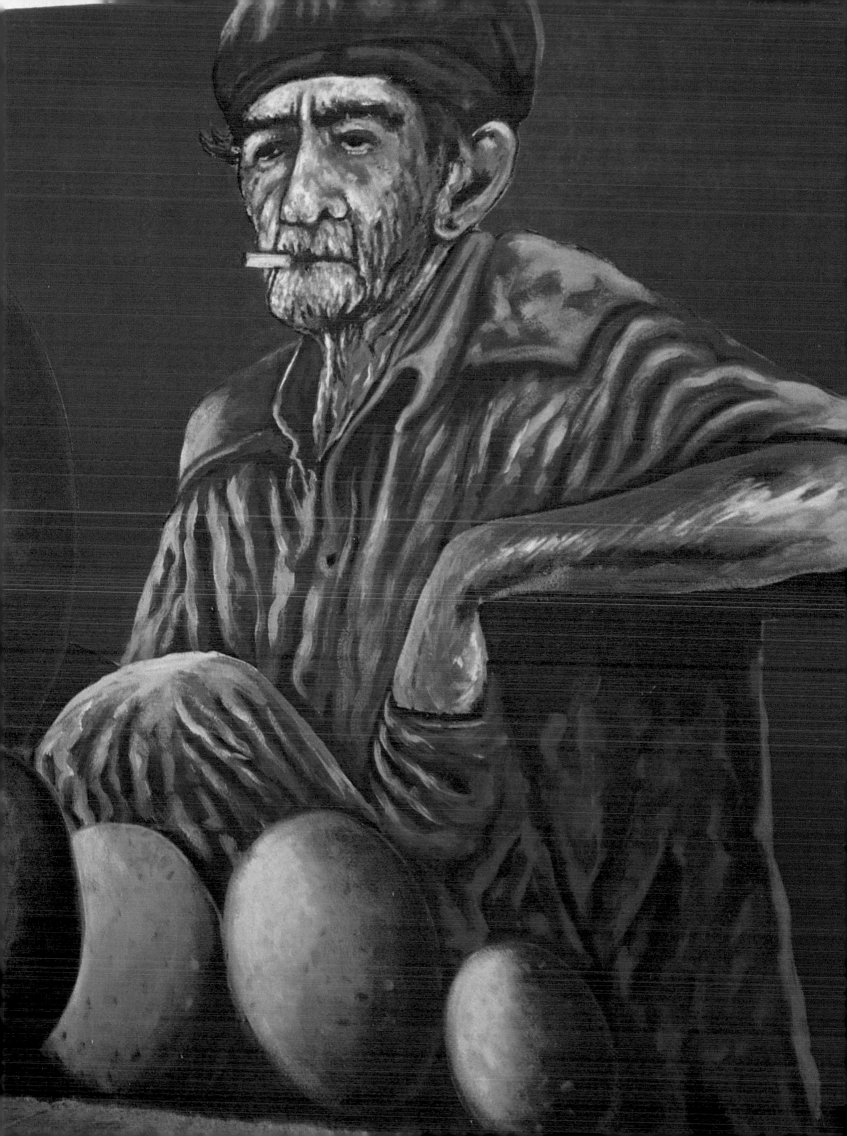

Santiago's Casa de la Trova is one of the most famous in Cuba, hosting performances by some marvellous musicians. Unfortunately, recent renovations have utterly destroyed its charm.
From their earliest years, young girls wear lipstick, use red varnish on their nails, and adopt coquettish hair-styles. This is all part of Cuban tradition. They are also likely to have their hair tinted.

candles, bunches of sunflowers, doll-like images of the Virgin, or pieces of copper. The red-domed, slender basilica, sited on an eminence, soars above the palm trees. This present shrine was constructed in 1927, and its appearance is incredibly colonial. The Virgen de la Caridad, carrying the infant Jesus in one hand and a golden cross in the other, became Cuba's religious patron in 1916. In the first decade of the seventeenth century, her wooden statue had been found floating on the waters of the Bahía de Nipe, south-east of Holguín. Since then, El Cobre has become very much a Cuban version of Lourdes. Crowds of the sick and infirm come to the basilica as pilgrims, hoping to be cured, offering the Virgin whatever they can afford. You can see the gifts they leave: balls, toys, bicycles, radios. Ernest Hemingway himself, already sick, offered the medal awarded by the Swedish Academy when he won the Nobel Prize for Literature. The Virgen de la Caridad is worshipped by Christians and devotees of *santería* alike. In the pantheon of *santería* divinities, she goes under the name of Ochún, as sensual as she is beneficent.

In the days when Cuba was America's favourite holiday spot, millionaires would hop into their private planes to fly from Florida, only a stone's throw away.

The sands of
VARADERO

Cayo Largo is situated 115 kilometres (72 miles) east of the Isla de la Juventud (Isle of Youth). Its total length is 25 kilometres (16 miles). The sand is white, the water turquoise. Cayo Largo is a diver's paradise, with coral reefs and sunken galleons. It is also ideal for pleasure-boating. This Eden-like island has a number of scattered tourist complexes; the total number of rooms in each is never more than 100, all with a sea view.

Once upon a time, America's high society would head for the most popular peninsula of the Antilles, Hicacos, whose reputation depended largely on its chief resort of Varadero. There they descended on the great luxury hotels like the Hilton, or vacationed on their private estates. In Miami, the advertisements in travel agency windows were the stuff of dreams – Marilyn Monroe lookalikes with coppery suntans and canary-yellow bikinis against backgrounds of palm trees and blue skies. Today the little strip of white sand, barely 19 kilometres (12 miles) long and 800 metres (875 yards) wide, attracts a huge number of tourists. The number of hotels is excessive – and still keeps on growing. Varadero looks like a permanent building site. Yet this has not always been the case. The place was put on the map once and for all by Irénée Du Pont Nemours, who bought land near the sea for a song and built a splendid colonial mansion on the beach. This is Xanadú – seen from the sea, it looks like a ship. The house has now become a plush restaurant, but has lost none of its magic and charm, with its terraces overhanging the roaring breakers of the Atlantic. It is easy to imagine the glittering balls and dinner parties the owners must

Cayo Coco, north of the town of Morón, is witnessing the growth of new tourist complexes. The island is 37 kilometres (23 miles) long. Cayo Guillermo is a tiny cay of only 13 km² (5 sq. miles), specializing in deep-sea fishing.

have given, and the house still seems to throng with the ghosts of characters straight from the pages of Scott Fitzgerald, in their long, silk dresses and alpaca dinner jackets. The story goes that the Du Pont family would turn up at the house without warning; just in case, the staff were expected to prepare a meal every evening for at least half-a-dozen people.

Then came the hotels, the casinos, the nightclubs, dance halls, and golf courses. Varadero's big occasions were *the* places to be seen. Swarms of young 'actresses' descended from all over the island, besieging the streets and hotel lobbies, commandeering the limousines. The Mafia infiltrated every kind of business activity. This went on for a good twenty years, with crowds arriving from Europe and South America.

Then came the Revolution. With it, the private beaches were collectivized, the casinos shut down. The golf courses were abandoned to the wilderness, the cabaret dancers sent home. The army of nymphets was 'invited' to help with the cane harvest. A handful of

hotels – the most ugly ones – remained open for the communist nomenklatura from countries with kindred ideologics. So things stayed for three decades. Yet history has its twists and turns. When the old Soviet bloc disintegrated, and Cuba was forced to look to tourism for survival, thoughts were neccssarily directed towards the restoration of this former paradise resort, now looking much the worse for wear. The work took place quite swiftly, with the aid of joint Spanish–Canadian investment companies; they soon erected new, palatial hotels, monuments to the glory of the tourist and the dollar. An international airport was opened – now you could land directly at Varadero, bypassing Havana. But the good-time girls began to flock back, and before long it was the old days again. For a few years, the *paladares* flourished, and every villa became a guest-house. The bars overflowed, the dancers poured back to the discos. The little town of Varadero resumed its previous incarnation as a twentieth-century Gomorrah, while Western magazines thrived on the scandals.

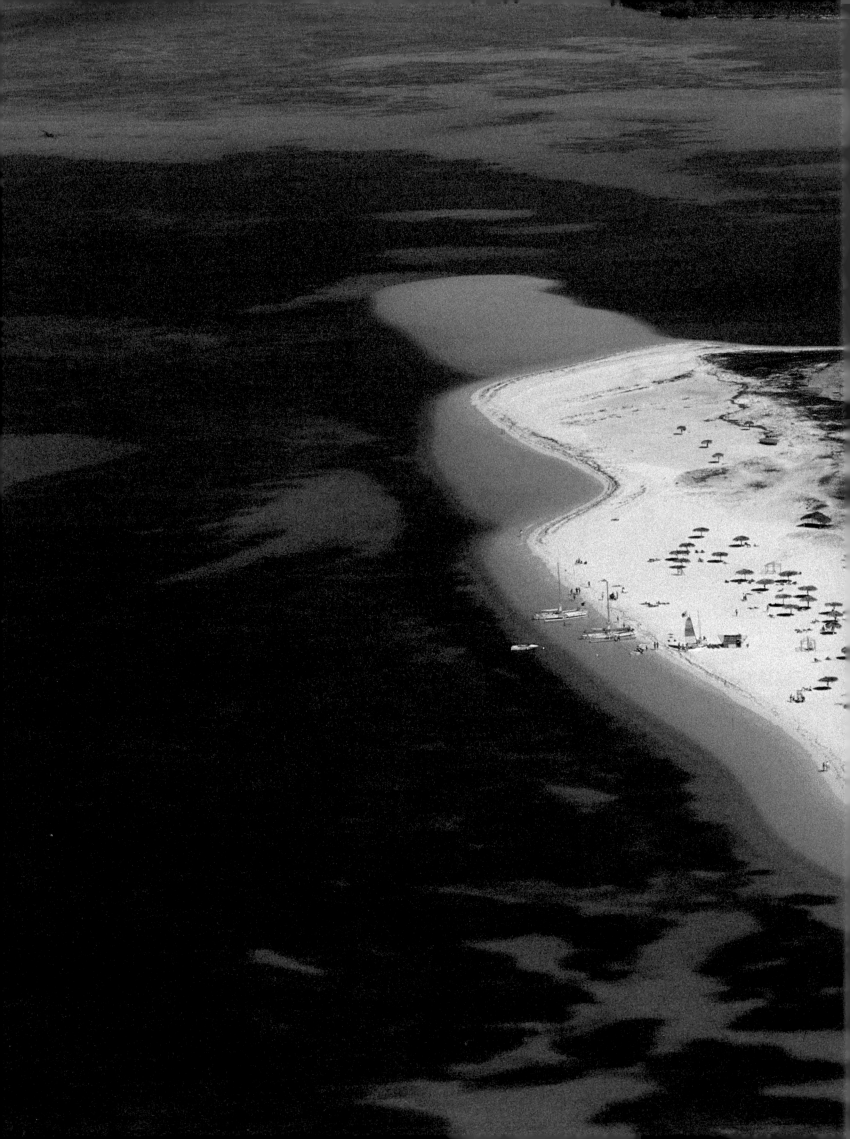

Suddenly, orders went out from the very highest level. An immediate and brutal stop was put to this drift towards the worst excesses of capitalism. All private establishments were closed. Special privileges were granted to hotel complexes operating package schemes, to state-run restaurants, and visitors travelling as groups or families. Gomorrah turned into a virtual ghost town, with police at every street corner and the holiday-makers segregated in their little air-conditioned paradises. Paradoxically, Varadero took on some very American characteristics. An amusement park was built with theme restaurants, a pool, shops selling local artefacts, and boat trips.

Enthusiasts of beach activities, sunbathing, water sports, and diving will find conditions largely unspoilt by mass tourism. The hotels grow bigger and better, like the Meliá Varadero or the Club Méditerranée, and the average holiday-maker does not go far from pool or terrace. Today the majority of Varadero's visitors come to laze around in a resort atmosphere which other destinations in the Antilles will find hard to beat.

Hicacos Peninsular is Cuba's oldest resort area – dating from 1872 and its most prized. Along its length stretches Varadero, where locals and tourists mingle.
Overleaf: Santiago has been a busy port for five centuries. Its dockyards, oil and sugar refineries, and rum distilleries are vital to the city and its surroundings.

USEFUL INFORMATION

TOURIST INFORMATION IN THE UK: Cuba Tourist Board, 167 High Holborn, London WC1 6PA; tel. 0171 240 6655, fax 0171 240 6656. Internet address: www.cubaweb.cu.

TOURIST INFORMATION IN CUBA: Corporación de Turismo y Comercio Internacional, Calle 23 entre 15a y 17, Reparto Siboney, La Habana; tel. (00 53 7) 336006, fax (00 53 7) 336046.

ENTRY FORMALITIES: Tourists require a passport valid for at least six months and a tourist card. This is available from your tour operator or direct from the embassy, and allows you to stay for up to 30 days.

CUBAN EMBASSY IN THE UK: 167 High Holborn, London WC1 6PA; tel. 0171 240 2488, fax 0171 836 2602.

BRITISH EMBASSY IN CUBA: Calle 34 no. 708, entre 7ma Avenida y 17-A, Miramar, Havana; tel. (00 53 7) 241771, fax (00 53 7) 2481094.

HEALTH AND INOCULATIONS: No special inoculations are required for Cuba, though some doctors will advise precautions against Hepatitis A, typhoid, polio, and tetanus. Do not drink tap water, and avoid shellfish as they have often not been properly refrigerated. Be advised that you may need to bring your own supply of regular medecines.

MONEY: The unit of currency is the peso ($), divided into 100 centavos. Cuban currency may not be imported or exported. Tourists use US dollars for most payments; you may receive dollar certificates in your change, which are worthless outside Cuba but can be changed at the airport. Travellers' cheques and credit cards are accepted as long as they have not been issued by US banks, such as American Express and Citibank. It is advisable to keep small amounts of *pesos Cubanos* for toilets, buses, phones, and minor purchases. But there is little use for large amounts of this currency, unless you are self-catering or going off the beaten track, and even then change only minimal amounts. There is also the *peso convertible*, which, unlike the *peso Cubano*, is on par with the dollar and valid everywhere.

CUSTOMS REGULATIONS: Items imported for personal use are not subject to duty, and you may also import up to 2 bottles of alcohol and 200 cigarettes. Other items worth up to US$ 1,000 may be brought into the country subject to payment of duty. Fresh foods and weapons may not be imported.

GETTING TO CUBA: The national airline is Cubana, whose address in the UK is 49 Conduit Street, London W1; tel. 0171 734 1165, fax 0171 437 0681. The airline operates flights from London and Manchester to Havana. Other airlines serving Cuba include Air France, Air Jamaica, Iberia, Mexicana and Aeroflot; the flight takes about ten hours. There are also airports in Varadero, Ciego de Ávila, Holguín, and on Cayo Largo. An airport tax of US$15-20 is payable. Individual holidaymakers are required to show a return ticket on arrival and to state the address of at least one hotel where they will be staying.

THE COUNTRY AND THE PEOPLE

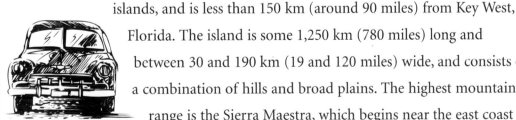

GEOGRAPHY: Cuba is the largest island of the Greater Antilles, located in the Caribbean right on the tropic of Cancer. It has several thousand offshore islands, and is less than 150 km (around 90 miles) from Key West, Florida. The island is some 1,250 km (780 miles) long and between 30 and 190 km (19 and 120 miles) wide, and consists of a combination of hills and broad plains. The highest mountain range is the Sierra Maestra, which begins near the east coast and is the most densely vegetated area of Cuba. Coffee and cocoa are grown here, and the highest mountain is Pico Turquino, 1,974 m (6,476 ft). The Cordillera de Guaniguanico in the west of the island reaches a height of 652 m (2,150 ft); a typical feature of its landscape are bizarre steep-sided limestone outcrops known as *mogotes*. These are scattered across the fertile Vueltabajo valley, where the world's best tobacco is grown. Most of Cuba's rivers are short and slow-moving, often running underground and, in the Viñales valley, forming caves. The longest river is the Rio Cauto in the east. Royal palms up to 24 m (80 ft) high dominate the landscape.

AREA: About 111,111 km² (42,900 square miles), just under half the size of the UK.

CAPITAL: Havana (La Habana), population around 2.1 million.

FORM OF GOVERNMENT: One-party socialist republic since 1959; direct elections introduced in 1993. The head of state is Fidel Castro Ruiz.

ECONOMY: State-owned. Cuba has been subject to a US trade embargo since the 1960s, and lost its main trading partner when the Soviet Union collapsed. The government sought to combat the economic crisis by opening Cuba up to tourism, now a fast-growing sector which provides a main source of foreign income. The main exports are cane sugar, rum, cigars and crayfish.

CLIMATE: Tropical: the most popular time to go is in the dry, cooler season, from November to April, when the average temperature in Havana is 20-25°C (68-77°F). Water temperatures range between 24° and 28°C (75° and 82°F) depending on the season. Humidity is very high during the rest of the year, and the rainy season lasts from May to October. Hurricanes sometimes occur in October and November.

LOCAL TIME: Five hours behind GMT.

POPULATION: 11 million, of whom approximately 70% are white, 17% mixed-race, and 12% black.

RELIGION: 40% of Cubans are catholics, 3% are protestants, and 49% have no religion. Also widespread is *Santería*, an Afro-Caribbean form of worship involving the conflict between good and bad spirits. Most Cuban families have their own small shrine in their homes.

LANGUAGE: Spanish. English is also understood in the main cities and tourist areas.

TOURIST ATTRACTIONS: The old city of HAVANA, with its beautiful squares and colonial buildings, has been declared a world heritage site by UNESCO. The city was founded in 1519, with fortresses (including Havana's trademark, the Castillo del Morro) being built to protect it against pirates and freebooters. The PLAZA DE LA CATEDRAL is the centre of Havana, and a popular meeting place; the Baroque cathedral housed Columbus's tomb from 1795 to 1898. Also worth seeing is the wooden paving of the PLAZA DE ARMAS outside the CITY MUSEUM, whose courtyard contains a statue of Columbus.

The FINCA LA VIGÍA to the south of the city is where Hemingway lived and worked for many years; today, his lovingly restored house is a museum. In the district of VEDADO, the streets are laid out grid-fashion, with the very long main shopping street of LA RAMPA leading to a seafront promenade lined with old villas, the MALECÓN.

Cuba's western province of PINAR DEL RÍO is a tobacco-growing area with a rich flora and fauna. The SOROA mountain region with its famous 22-metre (70-ft) high waterfall EL SALTO, and its orchid garden containing more than 700 species, has been declared a biosphere reserve. A visit to one of the cigar factories in the city of PINAR DEL RÍO is a must.

The main modes of transport in the sleepy town of CÁRDENAS are horse-drawn carriages and bicycles. The first town to be captured by revolutionaries in 1958 was the provincial capital of SANTA CLARA, some 300 km (190 miles) from Havana, and its MUSEO CHE GUEVARA is dedicated to the freedom fighters. Near the city, on a high plateau covered in pine forests, is the 30-km (19-mile) long HANABILLA reservoir, a paradise for anglers.

The stylish city of CIENFUEGOS, with its broad streets, was founded by settlers from the French colonies in the seventeenth century, and is known as 'the pearl of the south'. Famous performers including Caruso and Sarah Bernhardt appeared at its neoclassical theatre, the TERRY. The Moorish-style PALACIO DEL VALLE is now a restaurant.

The town of TRINIDAD, founded in 1514, stands on a hillside at the foot of the Escambray mountain range. The beautifully preserved colonial town centre is full of elegant villas in pastel shades of yellow and blue, built by former sugar barons, and is a UNESCO world heritage site.

Cuba's centre of culture is the provincial metropolis of CAMAGÜEY, famous for its *tinajones*: large, fat clay jugs placed beside people's front doors or on patios to catch rainwater. The natural history museum in HOLGUÍN has a very large and beautiful collection of snail shells.

BARACOA, at the far eastern end of the island, on the edge of the Sierra Maestra, was Cuba's first town; Columbus landed here in 1492. Further to the south is SANTIAGO, the most lively and Caribbean of Cuba's cities. Fidel Castro proclaimed the victory of the revolution from the blue balcony of the town hall overlooking CÉSPEDES PARK in 1959. The CASA DIEGO VELÁZQUEZ, with its carved wooden ceilings, is Cuba's oldest house, dating between 1516 and 1630, and is now a colonial museum. The CASTILLO MORRO now houses a museum of piracy.

The long sandy beaches of VARADERO, on the HICACOS peninsula some 144 km (90 miles) east of Havana, were very popular with rich Cubans and Americans at the turn of the century; Al Capone had his summer residence here. Today, it is a holiday paradise and tourist centre.

The island of CAYO COCO is covered in mangrove swamps and coconut palms, and is home to countless species of birds, including the *coco*, the small white heron after which the island is named.

TRANSPORT: Car rental companies have offices in all the main tourist centres, and often in hotels. Fully comprehensive insurance is compulsory. The main highways are often almost empty, and are well maintained; petrol is fairly widely available, but you should still plan where to fill up if travelling outside the main towns and cities. Local bus services are limited and often very overcrowded, though long-distance ones are air-conditioned and more comfortable.

There are also train services between Havana, Pinar del Río, Santiago de Cuba and Cienfuegos, though these are unreliable, dirty and uncomfortable. In addition, there are relatively good and inexpensive domestic flights linking Havana to the other four airports on the island; the flight from Havana to

Santiago, for example, takes only an hour and a half.

One of the most distinctive and attractive sights on Cuba's streets are the many 1950s American limousines, often used as taxis. Finally, cycle-taxis and horse-drawn carriages are common in many cities.

ELECTRICITY: Most hotels have 110-volt sockets, so you will need an adaptor.

CUBAN CUISINE: The food in Cuba is a mixture of Spanish and African influences. Dishes are often served with *arroz moro*, rice and black beans. Delicacies include fresh fish marinated in rum, and garlic soup; when in Pinar del Río, don't miss *cerdo asado*, suckling pig roasted in a wood oven. Whet your appetite with one of the many rum-based cocktails, such as a *mojito* (Cuba's national drink, typically flavoured with lime and mint), and end your meal by indulging in a small *café Cubano* and a Havana cigar.

Although all information was carefully checked at the time of going to press (February 1999), the publisher cannot accept any responsibility for its accuracy.